IF BY SONG

Marcia Karp

If by Song

LILY POETRY REVIEW BOOKS

Copyright © 2021 by Marcia Karp

Published by Lily Poetry Review Books
223 Winter Street
Whitman, MA 02382

https://lilypoetryreview.blog/

ISBN: 978-1-7347869-7-2

All rights reserved. Published in the United States by Lily Poetry Review Books.
Library of Congress Control Number: 2020949758

Cover Design: Martha McCollough

Acknowledgments

Grateful acknowledgement is due to the following publishers for previous appearances (with some few minor changes, including to titles) of particular poems:

Agenda: "Call for the Child, Call for the Dame"

Catullus in English (Penguin Books, 2001): "Brother"

Compost: "Come On Aphrodite"

Filled with Breath (Exot Books, 2010): "The Lover Resorts to Commerce"

Free Inquiry: "Of Fools," "What is Left"

Harvard Review: "My He"

Irresistible Sonnets (Headmistress Press, 2014): "The Lover Resorts to Commerce"

Joining Music with Reason: 34 Poets, British and American, Oxford 2004-2009 (Waywiser, 2010): "Evening Dance Class," "*Katastrophe*" (under a different title), "Brother," "*Ad Libitum*," "Tabula Rasa," "Mercy," "It's Showtime," "Erratatum," "I Won't Mind It Then"

Lily Poetry Review: "Oh, I Was a One," "Odd Little Woman," "If by Song, Words"

Literary Imagination: "They Are Not Us, Nor We, Them," "*Here*," "Dumb Show," "Most Dear and Most Due Ben. Jonson," "Sentence," "Now I Lay Me"

Literary Matters: "The Good Man"

New Ohio Review: "My Chance," "Song for the Returning of the Year"

Oxford Magazine: "*Ad Libitum*," "Beheld"

Partisan Review: "Brother"

Petrarch in English (Penguin Books, 2005): "The Lover Resorts to Commerce"

Ploughshares: "Familiar Rhymes"

The Poetry Porch: "Aprill," "What's Left of You," "A Lover's Spell," "This Mask. This Figure. Such Stuff."

Pusteblume: "An Horatian Toast," "Ranking Aemilius"

The Republic of Letters: "All Gone" (under a different title), "House Keeping"

Seneca Review: "If Asked, She Says Only," "Tabula Rasa"

The Times Literary Supplement: "The Human Female," "Don Juan in Hell"

Umbrella: "Erratatum"

The Warwick Review: "The Poet, David Ferry"

The Word Exchange: *Anglo-Saxon Poems in Translation* (Norton, 2010): Exeter Book Riddles 42, 54, and 86

With gratitude and lasting affection, these are those to whom my work is indebted: David Ferry, George Kalogeris, Christopher Ricks, and Rosanna Warren – and Ted Richer, who, first and last, has suffered the chips of my workshop

In memory of my family

Contents

1 Enmity

5 If Asked, She Says Only
7 House Keeping
8 There i was
9 After All Is
10 The Human Female
11 All's Fair
12 The Terms of Endearment
13 The Lover Resorts to Commerce
14 All Occupation
15 Aprill
16 Soon, I'll
17 My Chance
18 Having Been Given, upon the Prospect of Renewed Pleasure, the Date for His Departure
19 Now the City Prepares
20 By a Decision
21 *Here*
22 From the Oral Tradition
23 A Lover's Spell
24 Dumb Show
25 My He
26 These Two
27 I Find in My Arms
28 Song for the Returning of the Year
29 It's Showtime
30 Don Juan in Hell

31 I Won't Mind It Then

35 Erratatum

36 Most Dear and Most Due Ben. Jonson

37 With Thanks for the Ransom, *Selected*

38 The Poet, David Ferry

40 Poem in a Cramped Hand

41 And Forgotten

42 *Ad Libitum*

43 Tabula Rasa

47 They Are Not Us, Nor We, Them

48 Oh, I Was a One

49 What is Left

50 Mercy

53 Odd Little Woman

54 She

55 Call for the Child, Call for the Dame

56 One of Life's Mysteries

57 This Mask. This Figure. Such Stuff.

58 It Would Matter

59 Beheld

63 What better than words put in the ear at close range

64 Perverses

65 The Good Man

66 To a Friend, Some Days after a Disagreement

67	Miney, Mo
68	Dear ———,
69	An Apology
70	O Lucky Me
71	Apology for an Ancient Aftermath
72	Of Fools
73	Hello? Okay. Okay.
74	From on the Strand

77	What's Left of You
78	Now we're in the center: Adagio, *Don Quixote*
79	Just a Flick
80	Evening Dance Class

83	If by Song, Words

89	Exeter Book Riddle 42
	[I saw, at foreplaying, two wondrous ones]
90	Exeter Book Riddle 54
	[A boy came walking to where he knew]
91	Exeter Book Riddle 86
	[Many men were sitting]
92	All Women Know
93	Daphne
94	Come On, Aphrodite
95	Like *Phainetai Moi*
96	An Horatian Toast
97	There Once was a Man from Verona
98	Ranking Aemilius

101 Brother
102 Missing Brother, Missing Son
103 For Them and Their Son
104 Sentence
105 *Katastrophe*
107 All Gone
108 Song Sung after a Dirge
109 The Keys and My Mother
110 You May Have the Body
111 Familiar Rhymes
112 What You Did
113 Us Out
114 The family of Karp ran a school for itself
115 The House in Repair
117 Now I Lay Me

Enmity

The sculptor does not contend with the word,
nor the poet hate the stone.
But the pit within each word – oh,
that, may I have the stomach to corrode.

If Asked, She Says Only

If asked, she says only
    "I am no one."

Not wily, this answer –
    not wholly.

She says all the eyes
    have closed to her;

Without them she is no one
    to herself.

But it's only her self
    she has wiled,

For she knows who she is
    and can't bear it –

She is just who she meant to be –
    beguiling and

Shy of those eyes
    that adore her.

    Then her own
whirl in their tearpools,

    Taking
too long to return,

    So the other
feels lost and uncourted

    And she calls herself
only some no one,

    Blinding
hundreds of eyes

    Which had recognized
someone long since in need of some home.

House Keeping

The keeping of this house has nothing to do with love.
The window shades are drawn at dusk, rolled up again at dawn.
The sheets are changed each Sunday night. Bread is baked each Sunday night.
Sunday night the lists are made, the money drawn on Monday.
Each night the bedroom door is shut against the prowling cat
Who's well-behaved except at dawn. The dishes from the day
Are washed each night. Friday morning garbage goes; paper, tins,
And glass, each second Friday morning. Mornings, half a tin
And water, evenings, water, half a tin of cat food. Wash
The tin and put it in the thumbtacked sinkside bag. Pay bills
The Thursday just when due. When drawing money Monday,
Move savings-money into checking. Items on the lists
Are checked when done, and exed if not, then copied to a list
Of undone items. An item exed for two weeks must get done
Or … No penalty has yet been found which gets an item done.
All day Wednesday think of love. Feel unloved each day at dusk.
Saturday wonder where time's flown. Fly off the handle Tuesday
On the bus. Brush the cat and take a bath Saturday or Wednesday.
The rituals in this house have nothing to do with love.
The toaster must be watched. The kitchen floor is swept each day,
The windows washed each spring. Each spring others manage love.
The rugs are vacuumed twice each month, the curtains washed by boiling.

There i was

There i was   in a light drizzle   reading your letter to me
you felt sorry for me   you'd been willing to give it a go again
but i was too warped to let myself be loved by you
so you were forced by me to give it up
to agree that my leaving was just the thing   and too bad for me
it was flotsam   your letter   fished out of the storm in my basement
but the gift of warm rain followed the cold   and i read as if it were june
late into the night   outside with the stink of the refuse wrapped close for comfort
i read familial papers   and letters from others than you   and yours
when you thought i was special and yours
and that one when i had hurt you by leaving
how you'd been my greatest friend   and now i was lost

That time of saving and tossing   i kept the postcards
from china you'd sent   but that letter   i tossed it onto the flood
and only after   did i remember i hadn't been weak to leave you
or in need of fixing   or even   all these you'd said
about to be foundered without you   though it hurt now   a lifetime later
to read that i'd been at fault   and believe how bedraggled a catch i'd been
when you found me   i had a way to stop hurting now
as i hadn't all those times then   when i sobbed from your cruelty
because you could be kinder than anyone   and fun in your knowing so well
that you hardly were fun   and endless in bed
for you had a gift of not aiming to climb out of the valley of steep sides
but to wander at will   yours or mine   were the same will at those times
i remembered that you too were human
and had never wanted to bring me to sobbing day after day
you couldn't help it   but i wasn't so sad as to take much of you
though your kindness made me take some   and you could laugh

As we tried to shake each other out from under the skin
where we'd lodged each so firmly   each time we'd   as if nipping a flea
lighten the poison   you had another ex-wife to confess you'd kept from me
and a monkey who'd been a companion too

You lived as i imagine a monkey might   impatient of zippers and order
raging as if the insatiable itches you scratched made you the king of the jungle

After All Is

In the end of the light,
in my dim eyes,
you were a tender species.

Your forward limbs
pulling your back flat as it could ever be
you bared yourself and prepared yourself for me

who history swallowed.

I was only woman waiting for man –
Culture unheard of
but what a wasteland!

Twilight birds sang us into night.
We tensed and stretched and met and laughed.
If you were a species, I was its female.
And the sweat poured from our almost hairless carcasses.

The Human Female

It is not the first choice of the human female
To lie with her head on a cat – a Buck or a Minny –
Holding the weight of her head hard against gravity
Not to crush the kitty-cat overly
Much – the cat, less a pillow than underside blanket,
Not pleased into purring by the arrangement but curled-up
And lazy to change its position. The neck of the human
Female, grown tired in suspension, leads its head to a pillow
Of down – dead duck feathers – and down on the pillow
The head of the woman remembers she sleeps by a cat.
It has been years since a man shared her bed or his chest for her pillow
Upon which she had feared to place all of the weight of her head.
She had once had two cats, now she has one – fast asleep.

All's Fair

Rather would I be your love,
Not be alone in loving you.
Well, not alone: another does
And you, too, her, to whom you're true.

Alone, that is, without your love,
Though glad I am that you are true
When once you love. But why not twice?
You didn't wait, as I for you.

It's hardly fair. I've had no chance,
While she's had years and years of you.
You cast a part I never read;
You cheated then, oh cheat again.

The Terms of Endearment

When he, lent unknown, back to his lawful
and she, to her lone, go, time takes its toll.
                    ...
She finally sums in the prior earnest;
she figures the present harm, though error
remain hidden.
            On balance, she wants to
think the deal with him, with herself, is off.

The Lover Resorts to Commerce
To ———

Not, Oh not by me shall you get fame.
I will not line, O love, this box with you.
My lips are brazen, dustless, Delphic, warm,
While yours sprout veins of cobalt blue, and cold
Your eyes to match your stones. A crusted sac
Your heart, your head, your hair unwired is.
If I a rosebud, lush plush red red, am,
You, a fusty muffled ointment-daubed worm, are.
Your fingers, though they're ten, can't sum love's knot.
I'll carry not, O love, to fame your name.
I'll praise a tomcat (though unstoned), swiss cheese
(Though partial), Bromsgrove poems (although no though).
    Yet if you spend with me the course of sluttish time,
    And love me night by night, Oh, then what I will write!

All Occupation

She knew it was love – the twitch of arrival,
the twinge on departure, hours with his name
on the flesh of her tongue. Nothing the same
since she'd met him. Accepting no rival
who'd love her, her new love's survival
was all occupation. She must stay aflame,
for he had no part of it, never came
to her dead lips for his own lips' revival.

So long she kept love for that time-marking man.
Kept it so well that she mastered the art
and dared to discount him. Then new love began –
the twitches and twinges now messily real
to a man who made room in his heart
for a love that was sure to be far from ideal.

Aprill

Hurrah! Hurrah! Spring is here
  Spring is here today
Hurrah! Hurrah! Let's all clap hands
  Spring is here to stay
                    BLK

    The privet early-leafed in sparrow
The buoyancy of bees fresh out of spring's corral
The monarch will to equal gravity
The blop in thrall to now upon
  The woman ready for the newly-gathered man

  He does not make his call, or sting, this week
  While life spreads wide its favors

Soon, I'll

Soon, I'll be telling you I love you,
And when I do, you mustn't mind.
You mustn't say *me too* as people do.

You might remember who I am, you might be kind.

It wasn't me who wanted you –
I'd see you, and you'd slip my mind –
But now I do.
    And soon, I know, I'll love you.

My Chance

It was just too difficult to continue wanting you,
and when another man presented himself,
here was my chance to stop thinking of you,
I thought, and though I think of you still,
I don't, now, every time I wake, every time I walk,
every time I kiss this man, or every time I think of you.

Having Been Given, upon the Prospect of Renewed Pleasure, the Date for His Departure

I wonder if our months of just tolerable propriety,
forced back on our commonplace selves,
and my finding (relief!) that I like you in fact,
have been leading, not to our coming return to abandon,
but, despite (if return be return) of insistent involvings, to the sequela –
you gone, the earth in its determined spinnings through space.

Now the City Prepares

Soon it will make a parade of his return

The calendars that very day
all will display the day he has arrived

Festal phones that he's not set a-jingle
will ring illusions of his ring

The air, coalescent, will beat He Is Back

Pomp plumped to guyed pomposity,
he floats amazed through warrenous roads
The children aim their stones as he bounds past

Released from souvenirs, the women twitch,
hopping shyly onto the trail once more

By a Decision
For Rico

It is another round of Metaphors,
so you and I sift through our lives for Subject.
I praise another man, who will leave unstaked
claims he cannot clinch, but you say *despair*
and suppose yourself into the ring with another
immortal.
         Yet I think of this other man's eyes
and the striated mounds they surmount –
how I had looked and looked and touched his face
and held off his kisses until we had reason to know
our terms of contending were high staked and matched,
until we must get to our corners.

Here

And even now, as his words sound for her
their several years together, she cannot tell clearly
if he's been mute (as she's thought) (as she thinks she's been)
or if she's been deaf to him, until now

When she read what he sent her from there
   I'm here, thinking of you
she thought she could hear him saying
   I'm breaking that vow with the other,
   and keeping the one we haven't yet made

She couldn't swear
that's what he said
but for a moment
she took it that way –
that there was love between them

From the Oral Tradition

It's not couth, it's not kind, your complaint.
And it's (this'll kill you) not clever.
It came as a proverb you wrote
in the hope ... of what?
That next time I'd swallow your line
(hook and sinker) and stomach your spilt (wah) milk?

A Lover's Spell

For TR

Those other fatal femmes (you know them) insisted on renown.
But who's to fly the rumor when my lover is spellbound?
"Have pity on the tree," you said. "In silence it falls down."

> Helen had her heroes
> Kleopatra kissed a king
> But "Marcia makes men mad"
> Is not a brag the children sing
>
> > So let M be for mmm
> > A for again
> > R, our discretion
> > C, charm and change
> > I is indulgence
> > Ahh, yet again

(Dear you, who understand the privacy of trees –
M is him elsewhere, is mustn't, is mute.
I am entrusting you for a witness.)

Dumb Show

It is because I dreamed of a leaving not sufficiently marked
and awake saw that the other was you and I was the I
that the pain of your leaving – not me, but here, so me – has begun.

Or was it the evening and into night's noon
of Roquefort and figs and you kissed, as you do, me too soon
(I kept, while you did, the brutal sweet pungent mash to myself),
of sex we've made to our liking, of little to say,
of snores and your not letting go and my thinking *it's only in this I can find him*,
of my asking about your plans and how you'll carry them out,
of your saying *with luck I'll see you Tuesday*
that commanded the dream to make me regret I hadn't called (a nighttime ago)
you unfair or unkind or had ever agreed that yours is a method sufficient
                                                            to mimic love?

My He

Once I was sad. Now I am glad you
wouldn't, or couldn't, because (you said) shouldn't,
and probably more. Because if you had,
now would be after the fact. Too sad
now would be. But I do (you don't ask)
have a he, with a wife of his own, and
he does when he can and will do again
when he wants, though (here's truth for you) though
I said I am glad, my he should be you.

These Two

What a pair
This practiced rogue and his part-time lover
They never talk of love

And now she wants to leave him
or thinks it right to leave him
She thinks that she should want to leave

She thinks about his wife

When pressed – "She'd be annoyed," he says
A shallow truth, she knows, and yet
he's told himself the same, she thinks,
as he's told her

He's had her here and there,
most often in the bed next to the books inscribed, she sees,
for piety from uncles to the girl who's now his wife

Seven years they've done this

To leave, since there's no love,
or stay? (Or if there's love,
they'll not say)

She leaves

Neither one'll say good-bye and take what leaving brings
This married man, this parted lover –
no more, nor less, a pair

I Find in My Arms

How have you come, now I find
upon deep sleep's long leaving,
to lie in deep hum in my arms?

I was tucked up, tight neatly,
and deep in my sleep must have
fitted my arms to sweet you –

sweet pet, who, until the light comes
and the order of life, make me your home –
not the man I've just left
nor the man still to meet I might love.

Song for the Returning of the Year

Be who, today, you were last year
Sing what cannot be unsung
Say I am to you most dear
Fix my name upon your tongue

When you ride your she today
Wish it's me that you hold tight
Tell the thing what you would say
If it were me you ride tonight

Think the world a better place
Because last year you sang my name
Cry that all life's now a waste
Because you won't see me again

When you ride your she tonight
On your escape from trusting arms
Stumble in your wonted flight
See everywhere your puny harms

In stars, in fields, in standing ponds
See back what you have given
Dullard light and spindly growth and
Scum no thing could live in

It's Showtime

Come on – see the woman who keeps to herself.
   There, right there, the standing-place woman

I saw her get kissed and she saw that I saw.
He wound up her hair. He commanded her jaw.
But she winked as I watched her allow him to brute her.
He didn't think if he might or not suit her.
   There, (my dear), she could withstand embrace

One tried behavior to coax her to knowledge.
She held out for love. She refused to acknowledge
His presents of mind. "Only these!" would she ask,
Blearing and smearing her COME … NO, GO mask.
   Wear, and tear, the demanding-face woman

The staging was stagnant – ONE WOMAN ALONE. STILL.
The one cue for some drama was scrawled on the playbill:
GET ANGRY. She rued it, but knew it was so:
The excitement of rage, or the self-keeping woe.
   Soon here (do you hear?), she'll take it ill and give chase

Don Juan in Hell

It's a thing nobody talks about,
or at least not many do:
he wants, and she will,
but he can't, and oh god
all the trying and faking
to hide that it's trying. He can't
forget it, and she wishes
he'd fix it himself
or leave off in shame
or learn to talk dirty
or credit her kindness to him,
but he just has directions to give
and is no longer the man
she agreed to.
                Then he says it's not her,
and he'll need some weeks to relax,
and it's always like this with a new one,
but meanwhile, if only she didn't take
such pleasure in the small things
at a time like this.
                Nobody says,
except for him, who never has nothing to say,
she mustn't let on –
though it's time after time –
the one thing they do well together
is ride in his car:
it's leather inside, with a champeen's kick,
and she's learned to hold it and scold it
on those small-time roads he thinks
make him a man of the people; while
he snoozes, his yak – yak yakking –
switched now into blustering snorts,
and his hand, on hers on the stick,
a weakling's and no great shakes
to her or the gearbox,
                          she can make the thing
walk, trot, and tittup, then rear up and charge,
and she whinnies full-throttle as the car hugs the roads.

I Won't Mind It Then

I won't mind it, if at the last I overhear in the room
"Will you, do you think, get another Marcia when this one is …"
because, no matter the quiet or the *not now, can't you see* that follows,
I would then be someone with someone who loves me enough
to want in the moment if appetite returns
that then, just then in mid-hum, I would die,
so we'd both – I'd be part of a both! – be sorry I was dead,
not wrung out of sorrow by the diapering,
slobbering, gibbering mess of the long overdue.

Erratatum

I knew a drummer when I was a girl
and he was a man, who told me his rattattattat.
They'd never had anything like me, he said,
– ensnared not from love, but from art – among their beaten men.

Though we kissed after hotdogs and tasted of mustard,
his rolls and his flams and his tattattattoos
never sounded between us – the girl from one side,
the man from the other, of town.

He's still a man, if still he is.
I'm now a woman in grief for her art.
My tittle, my jot, have been scraped from my song.
They are mine and are perfect.
Stolen, my least sheep, my grace-notes, my ruffles.

I've always remembered that man from our vinegar kiss,
and his report – not the first, but the first I'd heard,
as he brushed by in kindness my life – of unmuffled madness from art,
that, if I dare master the ratamacue, might be mine.

Most Dear and Most Due
Ben. Jonson

*The Latin poem by John Donne that graced
the first edition of* Volpone, *Englished*

If but what through your art you dare,
        our Poet,
          avocats
of laws of men and God
  dared example and follow,
we'd gather such fine lines, O,
       as would mend us.

But they can't (for the cobwebs) see
        the ancients;
         you, only,
dare hear, and make new, old clues.
Go catch a precious fly and weave
      a fox-trap. Do.

With threads grown gray, bind off the births
       of your books:
        the well-wrought
page can't be charted in half-pint lines;
and those books you wish to give [Lat.
  dare] perpetual life to
    ought be born old.

You cocker hard your genius up
     and live free,
      one among
the ancients: now go past those past to redeem
  (from out of our vice) a future
(our vice that here more habitually dwells
  than ever before and than will
    ever again).

With Thanks for the Ransom, *Selected*

A Poem for (though not about) a Friend

I hope I might learn from the timing
of sequent and alternate rhyming
and learn from the darkness he harrows,
and too, from the bland ones he troubles,
that poems thrive, we die, in narrows.

One room for one poem is pleasant
with change not of difference, but augment.
A life that does not change its patterns
has secrets sad, strange in their syllables –
his ringing clayed taciturn tuned bells.

The Poet, David Ferry

April 4, 2007; Boston

He had both a level broadness across his shoulders and a tallness,
so that when he changed his posture in order to lower his gaze,
creating the illusion that he was on our level,
though he was instead still over our heads,
now by some fewer inches, he did so by a torque
that raised his right shoulder and lowered his left.
It seemed so natural a posture to him, habitual,
as if he'd lived long in his full height among people much shorter,
among whom his disciplined inclination brought everyone comfort.
Being so broad, some part of him was still tall in his torque,
though his head was lowered by that kindness of his
that was one kind of talking down to us, but not another.

A listener needn't have known of the poet's recent catastrophe
nor have cared a fig for the life of the poet
in order to have trusted what he wrote in his own ways about the mundane
and, in the old ways, of lives that no one has or could really live,
unless it is that the ferryman of metaphor can
(and alone) from the jealous belly of time return
and return us, our mutilations now stanched,
for the moment, to any life whatsoever.

So when the poet brought over for us that old story
of how Hades whetted his own seasonal grief
on the moment of another's, because this time art came hard
and perfected on the heels of sorrow, we, too, fell for a moment
for the ruse. But that infallible assayer was only
setting his gold to spin, for the dizzying pleasure of pain.
He had to have known, he knew, the terms were all his,
that no husband who loved could but twist back and down
toward the wife he held onto tight, could but, for a second of comfort,
become the last death she'd suffer.

So then, when the gold on Mr. Ferry's finger came forward
as he accommodated to us by his diagonal bow, even those

who had had no clue, must have realized that the ring tolled the life in the song,
that was just then not an old one at all, for it looked, for all the world,
like the mouth of Orpheus still in its NO, or like the
bewildered path worn smooth by a dog in its faithful circle
on the trail for the scent of its mistress.

Poem in a Cramped Hand

In too early memory of the cat called Sika

I know a writer who,
were the arm under this cat his, and
just having found what he thought was a way
to make something of its bit-by-bit dying,
would then just throw off the animal,
so as to make his way back to his desk.
He'd not admit the hurt he'd caused
into his register of thought,
unless by that way his pages might be improved.

Time's anticipatory agent, he, would think only
of getting it right and of giving it an exact beauty,
so that that thing he was unmoved by –
this cat, whose subtractive way out of its life
could be made a fine figure –
might, in his very something, give life to him,
and hang him, there, in literature's gallery.

Self-portraits, all, whatever way an eye might look.

And Forgotten

Not my dead or the dead of your neighbors,
the dead of your youth or the dead the world mourns,
are honored as you would you'll be in your death

You've figured your way to meaning,
figured you've got it right,
having thrown out God and country
    suit and tie
    wine and roses and
    nice and easy

You've worn it away to *I know what and I know why*
But when you die, you'll be dead, and if read
and admired, there'll be – you know – other such, too

Ad Libitum

    I like the dark and the air through the window
and the lamp on its arm – the one outside
and the one by my right hand, clamped to the desk.
I like the breeze and the heat it doesn't displace.
I like the typing and wish it were writing,
and I don't care as much as I should.
I like the every-so-often confusion of sounds:
the chair being rubbed by the desk, the cat,
a night bird at the feeder, my stomach.
    I am pleased to roll to the reference book shelf
and pleased to pick, over there in the dark,
the right volume for "digestive." My guess
at the root was wrong: not *gusto* for taste,
but *gero* for carry. *Di-* for apart:
to tear, to divide. Authorities differ, but maybe
di-viduo, whence *widow, widower* –
to tear in the eye and the heart.
Still, words are not poems.
    What I would like now is to stop.
The typing is fun, but it is, after all,
writing I want. Still, I am pleased by the sound
and the move of the keys, except when they lock,
and the carriage is nice on its creak of return.
The keys have three greens, but it is writing I am after.
    I like its being my neighbors parking the car,
not strangers peering at lives behind windows,
some with screens on, but not all with them on.
I'll bet it looks romantic at this corner of a dark house,
a late night in June, the weather finally in season.
    I am grateful this house,
bequeathed by a family to me, its youngest –
now, only – has chairs and books all over,
so when and in whichever I want,
I may sit and read or sit and write or sit and sit.

Tabula Rasa

For one under erasure

I wrote the history of poetry
and prose. Of poesy and prosery
I wrote. Not all of it, just little bits
I chose, although I thought about what I'd
left out and wrote again and wrote some in.
I tried to write, in prose, what writers know
of craft. In prose go straight. But hesitate
in poems.
        Just like a child, my hands were drenched
in ink and paper balls of scrawling round
my feet were calling *Read me*. Some I'd read
again, and reading, knew that knowing prose
and poetry in history was far
from what I knew.
        My tongue, my English tongue.
I closed my eyes and closed my hands so I
might hear how English spoke on all those tongues.
And underneath the tongues there is a mind
that has no words. It's there that language is.
And that – above my English tongue, the his-
tory of poetry and prose, the po-
ems, prose, the knowing – that arose to call me. O.

They Are Not Us, Nor We, Them

As if we haven't wanted for ourselves their special gifts,
As if defiance were not in their falls,
They walk off branches, on, then off,
Upon, then boom, they drop, then walk upon our ground.

They laugh – cheep cheep – at our green eyes.

As if a magic hand sluiced round
And touched each one of them
A touch – please please – we each want aimed at us,
They up wheel gather fly bye-bye

From us who lumber in our jealous flight machines.

Then some of us are providence
And some boom of us provender.

Oh, I Was a One

Oh, I was a one who, had I but been there,
would have, I would have done, done all that doing
that would have been needed to be done.

Oh, I would have, I tell you, been the one to say –
No!, to do – the right and the noble.
Clean hands, oh, clean heart in my doing the deeds
for the land, for the folk, for the highest of reason.

Oh, I I I I, had I only been there.

Now here there's a wolf crying Wolf!,
sounding all about. Still, I raise no axe,
I raise no horn, I raise no cry to shout the chaos out.

Oh, how can I ever be face to my face again now,
knowing what I know I know about me?

What is Left

We think it is new. We are so, so afraid.
We think there has never been, ever been,
a thing like our thing. So, we are so afraid.

Just think.
A village rapes a girl.
A village burns a man.

Here is the maelstrom.
Here is the horror.
People we like are like people we don't.

It is our turn to live it and not know what hit us.
It is our turn for mayhem that droppeth as rain.
It is our turn to cry we are virtue's last bastion
while mayhem and *help us* turn us into them.

She is twelve and they rape that girl over and over.
That collar of tire, which then becomes fire,
is fitted by many hands to one neck.

Nobody taught us. We know how to do it.
We shout and we leap, for our lives, to some standing.
It is you. No, not I. Yes and *no no no. Help us.*

We say that that thing
is loosed
from another town over.

O tut tut. Just think.
It is ours and is us.

What is left for our thing when havoc's in swing?
    All against All
    First among None

Mercy

Did you know, do you remember now, "the rat race"? –
honest, disinterested God in that lab coat
and stinky meats to send us, amazed, ascurry.
The first shall be first and the last shall go hungry
or hang, was the theme. Not a god for all time,
that clipboarded watcher, and too antiseptic for ours.

Mounted now each on the god who is God of the gods,
the tune is "On Vengeance. On Destiny. Gee-hup."
and a brutal whip hand on the flank of each courser.
At the races, no doubts; and the rich have the right
of way and the poor are left the dust. Never mind.

One of the old gods was born as a winnow wind
and each of us blew toward some runnel to outrace the flood
of our lives. It was good for the gods and remains
so: the first should be best, for the rest are as beasts.

Odd Little Woman

The odd little woman doesn't know what to do.
When asked to partake, she looks round to see whom
you might mean and discovers there's no one but her.
Though she wants to say yes, she'll only demur.
She knows, when her best, her fuss is not right.
She can't tell if her handshake is limp or too tight.

She'd like to be family. She'd like to be friend.
She'd settle for species and fears she offends.
Yet there's nothing peculiar the others can see.
(It's gotten so she is embarrassed to be.)

She'd known joy as a child and remembered it when
she was loved and herself then, but not lately again.
She'd been loving to love of all kinds, so it grew.
Was it me, she wonders, or not, who withdrew?
It wasn't her plan to be so alone;
still, she is, like a creature that's fouled its home.

She

She'd been saying it for so long –
and with passion, too –
that there was a person inside every body,
that every person was as surely the world
as every other person was.
But when she lost any place she'd had in the world,
she knew it for sure,
and, since she'd always been able
to put to the side herself,
the sureness, seeking to find its level of change,
found a ground long seeded with shame
and flooded into flourishing such a harvest
of behind-the-scenes peerings that she knew herself
only desire clothed in legend,
in cunning, and in will, and in endless supply.
And she did her worst on herself
by doing her best to keep mum that she was.

Call for the Child, Call for the Dame

Shame is the name and rudimentary game
someone plays now with you.

                                            Call her to home.
If she comes at all, blamed-faced it is, absolving,
she would, crime-done by crime-claimed.

                                            Call her to task.
If she bears it at all, she'll cry, *why did I, why?*,
salting the docket to mush.

                                            Call her to arms,
where she'd like most to be, and so will have none.
She'd have you cradle no one.

                                            Call her to mind.
What a shame – what remains are the game and the name
and their claims.

One of Life's Mysteries

Hard to say if she was sent packing or if she went missing.

Here is the gist:
    Finally, the subject (at whom the instruction was aimed),
    breathing it out, said
    "No, not that, but this is the nature, the time, place, and name of the matter."
    The other (who would better her friend)
    (breathing in *this* for *that*,
    continued, blind to her swerve in the matter,
    knowing herself – so all evidence points –
    only always the deep one, the fact one, the keen)
    kept up the correction.

Here comes the crime:
    The subject lit out from the scene of the pinched inspiration
    or else she went dark to herself.

Write it up: erasure by pushing or – was it? – by jumping.

This Mask. This Figure. Such Stuff.

What is this mask I've grown?
It does not suit me at all.
It is cracked and worn. How could I know
This would be the mask I'd grow?
I have not reaped what I meant to sow
(In morning's dew, as I recall).
What is this mask I've grown?
It does not suit me at all.

Who cut this figure from such stuff?
It never could have been the mode.
Welts and clabber, who could touch
This figure? Who cut it from such stuff?
This warp is stretched, this weft is rough.
(This morning, I recall, it was finely sewed.)
Who cut this figure from such stuff?
It never could have been the mode.

What is this mask I've grown?
Who cut this figure from such stuff?
I recall mornings a fineness showed.
Not this figure. Not this mask I've grown.
No fine skin, no mornings, no dew, no fine bones
Have been left me. I've clabber and welts and dusk.
What is this mask I've grown?
Who cut this figure? And from such stuff?

It Would Matter

I was going, it was supposed, to have a child or more
who would look in the crook of my arm and wonder.
I might, I was told by the one whom I'd asked,
answer the questions by telling a tale of the dragon
who'd seized me when I was still young. I was burnt,
I might say, or enfanged, and must leave it at that
I was told, when I'd be asked, supposing a life I might lead.

It was I, silly me, who was led, by time, more than life,
I can say. I can say I stayed still and let time,
more than life, have its way through me. No one asked.
Not the lovers – not after the first,
who must have been drawn by the care I took in the hiding.
Not doctors or teachers or friends or the usually nosy:

not until Wednesday this week. I came along for the ride
with a friend to a man who studies scars and the truncated flesh
that holds them. He saw I'd been a child, or more,
and he let me be part of the day. I got to test the hook
soon to be a hand for my friend. He rolled up my sleeve,
placed the sensors, made sure I got that hook to close.
That's an old scar, he said. So, he saw me and knew
it would matter that I was a part of the day.

Beheld

When ugly woman catches sight of beauty in her face
and is thrown into gladness, mightn't even you feel inclined
to believe that optical imps on the other side of the glass
depict our backward world for us and, that what the woman sees next,
that beauty blurring, is the quivering in silly glee of the erring imps
enjoying the fast one they hadn't meant to pull,
not what she on her side takes for a folly made out through tears deeply drawn?

What better than words put in the ear at close range

You said, "close friends who for some time were cold" while we hugged.
I remember when the trees were dead and this was just a dream.
You said you'd begun to remember enough of me
to miss me, a close friend once, now in the cold.
"Bring me in out of," I know I meant to say.
Then I awoke and found it has stayed with me,
you saying those words I put in your mouth
in that hug of conspiracy I made up for us.
All week, those who want to and can
have brought to this winter-wrapped road
men and machines bringing bared trees to ground
and grinding the hidden green pulse to dust.
I'd be your friend again in a minute
if you would remember and miss me and tell me you do.

Perverses

It seems we must do it –
    tock a clock's tick
    wobble crickets' cricks
    hobble each straight course
    balk true friendship –
until lub dub grows weary,
    and stops.

The Good Man
For GK

It must have happened, Iorgas, to you –
You found yourself downstairs
one day in a child's game.
Your playmates were strangers to you,
you just realized, and then realized more –
you weren't that to them.

That had to have happened, but that's not my point, which is this –
You must have had, sometime during your games,
or on the way up the staircase, a feeling
to answer the one you'd first felt while you played.
The first was a strangeness
that you were known to these boys.
The answering feeling hinted you'd already met them,
hinted you'd been, before now, alive,
but you didn't know for sure or when.

That must have happened – didn't it ever – Iorgas, to you?
A tile from the vault of your infant's long-lost
came loose and left you somehow with words
to suspect today wasn't the first day
you'd been in the world, and these older boys
(your mother had said *cousins*), boys not yourself,
had seen parts of you you'd never know.

Our friendship has grown up, too –
When we first met, we were, of course, strangers,
and you were vague to me time after time.
So, by the time we were friends, we each (am I wrong?)
had to wake to the other, as if meeting just then not as strangers.
Through a clearing the size of an unmoored tile,
I'd glimpsed you, but darkly,
and had but a hint that my wide experience
would be your never-failing kindness and reserve
that no one but no one could miss,
not even, I wish it were so, you –
Iorgas, always yourself.

To a Friend, Some Days after a Disagreement

It seems when we met on the street
that you had forgotten who I was to you
as I had forgotten the same about you.

It was chance that we met, though I'd helped it along
having gone past your door. You were out. When I saw you
I stayed where I was. And just as I knew

you'd turn right and couldn't turn left,
I was sorry for you to see you were angry
but knew you'd be glad when you saw me.

You were and I was. We gladly shook hands.
You had to run. You told me where.
You said we'd soon talk. You admired my hair.

You looked at the book that I held. I showed you a crux.
We laughed – it was Greek to us both. And I knew, did you,
that years ago you'd admired my hair when worn up.

Miney, Mo

Come, let's play a dress-up game.

The most generous man in the world should be you,
and I your trencher-woman. I'll be
welcomed to scamp on your Tom Tiddler ground.

Let's play on our names. You get to be rich,
reeking with open hands-out.
Crapulent, me, on your offerings.

Let's play Just Rewards For Ingratitude
and laugh at my stuck mask of grasping.
You can be Civil and I can be Unctuous.

You? Brilliant. Me? Glaring.

Let's play Pick The Pockets Of You.

If the costumes fit, let's wear them. Oh, fun.

Come on. Now. I said you should play.

Dear ———,

I know a woman who knows she must not talk to you this way,
but her flaw is a pool, not a crack, of loss and
she'd draw from you more than anyone should if not stopped and
the shame of it is the terrible injustice to you,
who's been nothing but kind and kinder still,
when she uses that kindness to prime the world for yet more,
but it is not the world who must suffer her rage on the handle,
but you.

An Apology

As if to win high favor of my tutor
En explication de texte des hommes et femmes;
Secure my, loose the place of other students;
Show my lines well-considered, theirs ill-framed;
I praised each first (I meant the praise unclouded),
As: *Hers are rich in learning; His, in thoughts*
Profound. Fearful lest I be disallowed
My place then (or did I mean I ought not
Hide the scope with which I read the world?), I
Counted faults what I heard faults, I scanned
Too close, discounting faults of my dim eyes;
Then sprinkled down doubt on spite, and washed my hands
    Of what I'd done – the worst to you, to think
    You'd prize my lines, who write in honest ink.

O Lucky Me

Once I encountered,
O lucky me,
a man who would think.

I said, "Thinking Man,
will you think for me?"
His eyes were turned
and he would not encounter me.

I said, "Then, Thinking Man,
will you think with me?"
I guess he thought
and thought he would not.

Then I tried to think
and I did not know how
and I did not know what.

Now, once a year
I try again,
and what I think
is of that Thinking Man.

Apology for an Ancient Aftermath

This is a fissure so old
It hasn't got a name.
This is a crack along the bone of me –
So old, so deep to the marrow.

I stood, I wept from invective.
You couldn't hear what I heard
Spewed from the fissure – the marrow of me
Giving name, naming me.

These are the names got from the deep of me –
Shame and Shouldn't and Must.
Listen!
      You were only the needed jostle
That loosed the cracked tongue that judged me Awful.

Of Fools

I saw it that way from the couch –
    the many-masted ship of ivy in the bottle of the world
    with sprays of laurel rising behind –
as we argued the message of luck come to me,
for fortune had tost, this time, her waves my way.

Jealousy overwhelmed your staunchness,
then you overcounted the bounty.
And I, in pride of my quickness,
heaved the lead
and cried the soundings just ahead.

This extravagant season will unbound the wandering ivy.
A Jacko'all is on his way to cut the shrubs back and deft.
While we, knowing mainly one thing between us,
have already submerged luck's call to me and won't speak of it –
though we storm about the known and unknowing world –
ere acrimony end.

Hello? Okay. Okay.

This morning that sound in your voice let me know,
though you've never yet pulled off the counter-spy bit
[and you've never, I bet, thought that I
(who live on the qui vive)
find it love to be sent to pick up on the low-down
dropped in befuddled imbalance between
(as I lived it) me here and her there with you]
in which you coolly tip me off that you are,
as long as you keep her still willing and present,
an inside man in the house of love,
instead, you play yourself, a bumbler who,
having stumbled upon the fedoraed jinn's wish –
the quicksilvered figure shaped to a girl –
has been granted the second, an impossible, wish
of holding her held, as tit-tat for your signing
(yet always again) off on the Sucker's Agreement:
    This is (don't you know) your only chance;
    Let go of enthrallment (for even a sec) at your peril.

From on the Strand

Since – by now, don't we know –
when you go, you'll come back,
would you, next time you leave,
leave me word: *Me* or *You*?
Don't say more.
Don't explain.
It will help just to know
where the moon is each time
I am left high and dry,
phased out of your life
till you turn with a rush,
and I founder myself still yet deeper
into the muck that your undertow leaves,
unable to read you yet, unable to navigate.
Possibly yet on course.

What's Left of You

The way you have it,
you've hobbled the rabbits,
unshod the horses,
pounded to pulp all wood,
and steadied first stars.

Ah if, dear friend, it really is luck
that you command, we wish you might come with us,
on hands, on knees, when it is summer again,
into the lawn of impossible clover.

Now we're in the center: Adagio, *Don Quixote*

Here we can move   our arms through air
and here we can jump   as if we can   jump
There is a man whose arms were sawed off
There is a man with new arms sewed on

    Coupé devant
    Passé and reach
    out from the knee
    Now stretch   and point beyond the toes

    Trace with the wrists
    Let the hands weep
    up to the full
    Down   slow

He is a man whose legs were sawed off
He is a man you can't but think of
when your arms move   as if through thick air
your muscles firm   to make your arms float

        Here, now, the dance is sought
        The sawn-sewn man, there, must make his own way up
        If I am ever   to make the jump
        the floor   must let me up

Just a Flick

The others go twirling, like marbles set free
In the back of the room, I stand
The one who might watch them, the dancer, our teacher,
comes over and dances for me
He unturns those turns into steps I might do
and I watch without doing, stuck
in the kindness of one who can fly, who yet
leaves all the others and gives just a flick
to one who could never try

Evening Dance Class
For Debra

You forget you have told me this three weeks running, and
I can see you slower than the others,
afraid of putting the wrong foot forward
and back, to the side, tap the toe twice,
then the heel.

I see you stretching too long to the left,
palms down when they should be up,
the line of the newly enrolled moving here
and you still there.

I see the swell of your ankle and tears
and you, counting and keeping together
with the intruders as best you can,
ignored now, neither stopping nor dancing.

I can even see you writing your letter,
telling your teacher how hurt you are
to be now left behind.

But I can't, because you close the door and
play the music for yourself alone,
see you just later, in spin, in time, alone, in tune,
held up light and lithe by your wrists in graceful sweep, afraid,
in your dance, of no one and nothing.

If by Song, Words

I have no words.
I meant to have.
And then she thinks:
That's not just it. Not the truth.
Not words I lack, not first the words.
I have no thoughts,
so do not need those words I thought I would.

Once I thought I thought great thoughts:
I knew my dead. I knew my lost.
Seemingly…
I saw great sights. No one could see past me.
I…

An eye is not enough
An eye that keeps its pictures straight
An eye that names its colors

Upon the palette of my life
lie puddled mirrors mirroring me –
one color – me – mirroring me.
Always me the silenced lover
turning back to look too soon
    at me, the half-regained beloved.

Me and me sitting in a tree
No birds to sing us – tweet *– sweetly*

Her self's bells jangled out one tune:
    Unloved.
        Love
      me. Love
          me alone.

So she would not love the others –
Seeing only that her eye must

Then leave the face of her waters,
And leaving, leave nothing.

Without words she would propagate muteness –
Her tongue a dull fish without spawn.

Unmoved, her neck locked, looking
Into the watered eye: a blink,
Obliteration; a kiss, a drowning
Into self. But everything was.

    Ah, where was truth?
    She'd been awash with love,
    Held high above
    In Daddy's arms.
    Admired from below,
    Apple of his eye,
    Pink pippin.
    Fall for me, he said.
    Fall for me: the mother, too.
    Her world had rippled with love.
    I'll catch you
        You in my eye – love's old duet for three.
        Caught you.
        Got you.

    Riven with love
    She was so perfectly each of them –
    So as he was, so much was she as her.
    Their little girl – she had an I for everyone.

She didn't know the others though.
They are themselved, she said.
She said, *Completed, I am not.*
She said, *Completed. Whole.*
She didn't see the others how
(In mirrors speaking each
To each alone) they love.

There she sat
By the pool
    Sitting by the pool she watched her
Looking face
Never spy
    What she sat and watched there after
O mine eyes
You did lose
    Sight of sights which pain not, please me
Tweedledum
Kissed Tweedledum
    Tantalizing kiss and arid

If by song, words return,
The watch I keep I'll keep no...
But she could not say it.
    A bird, the wind, some tick-tock god,
        Touched the face of the water. She sang:
            They'd ridden on her tongue,
            Interfered with its calving,
        What are you talking? What foolishness talking?
            Each neophyte phoneme,
            By a pout, then a fuss,
            Was repotted by Daddy
            As a patho-phonus
            Or a paleo-phonim
            Save the girl graft the stem
            (Forget-notting the mother)
            With a hot-house phonem.

    And if this is so, *my tongue so phonumbed,*
    It also is so that the ocean can't drown.

    But, they
        Yes, but she
            And, then
                And again

    My tongue! it was flayed into floundering strips.
    It's mended.

And yet
    (How little she knows)
        they wanted me dumb.
No! they polished their pippin.
Ah! a pink little piglet in constant snuff for the truffle of love.

They made themselves mirrors. Their eyes were my pools:
Daddy's smart cookie…
And mother?
Mother heard my words as chimes.

Father Time sent Mother Tongue
To fetch a pail of water
   So she fetched the water's wet
   The water's face
   The deepy depth
   So she fetched the water's voice
In which they bathed their daughter

Ah, where is truth?
(Anchored at the mouth of the bay,
The ship of truth keeps raising its hull.)
Yes, she says, *I have words, but…*
(The mast-dove returns to report a port
Famous for laughter and little of self.
The anchor is weighed. Away!)
And then she sings: *And then she sings…*

Exeter Book Riddle 42

I saw, at foreplaying, two wondrous ones,
    at large, laid out for the looking.

The fairheaded fair will (under her whatnot) grow great
    if the work of their playing went well.

Now, by rounding my fresh-from-my-forge runic staves
    into the halls of your hearing

    (you wits of words and their works),
may I be sounding the names of these two to your knowing.

    Take from the CORN only its first crunch of sound.
    Take it twice. Take it thrice.

    Quit sitting. Quick. Pick INCUBATE's gift.

    One mate is complete with what AUSPICE can offer.

    With a CHIRP, the match (the set of the game) is dispatched.

Has anyone caught from my staves the key
    and been able to bear it
        to the guardings on the gates of the hoard
            and open the fastness as if flimsy hoarding
        then run through the ruin
    and bedevil the bonds round the heart of my riddle
which never before has lain bare?

    Now, we-at-our-wine can name
the foul-minded company we keep.

[A Cock and Chick]

Exeter Book Riddle 54

A boy came walking to where he knew
she would stand for what he would do.
He stepped from afar to her in that corner.
     His hand raised his shirt.
     He pushed under her skirt
his stiff I-know-not-what and he horned her.

That boy worked his will; they waggled together.
His good servant bestirred him and sometimes did help.
That strong handyman stopped, bedraggled, who'd wet her
     who'd only begun,
     though he'd come undone.

     Then there did grow
     in her below
what good men might hold dear and get by their wealth.

[A Churn]

Exeter Book Riddle 86

Many men were sitting
Wise and deep in thought
A thing came in to where they sat
Here are the things this thing has got

>One eye for its seeing
>Two ears for its sounds
>Two feet to walk round on around on its rounds
>
>Twelve wise men each counted
>Up ten heads times ten
>The heads are enough heads for twelve hundred men
>
>Two hands for its doings
>Two arms as is custom
>Attached to two shoulders from which it can thrust them
>
>One back and one front
>To hold it together
>One neck and two sides that keep out the weather

Tell me truly tell me do
The name I shall be called by you

[A One-Eyed Garlic Seller]

All Women Know

Young Cupid, cock not your bow with shafts of gold
nor lead. All women know it is not your arrow
that finds a man a bed. Become a shepherd
if you would know why she says yes and she
says no.
        All shepherds know the ewe will agree
if the ram is strong, and the ewe, for the moment, is free.

Daphne

He stalked me
Taller than me and looking down
And he thought we were friendly

I ran for my own sake
Yet he asked me to slow down
Then I got to some water
And I stayed on its shore

It nourished my feet
And it gave me a rest
And my arms turned to limbs bearing limbs

He stood in my shade
And he sang me my song

I grew my hair proud
And the sea bathed my feet

Come On, Aphrodite

from Sappho

Aphrodite, beauty queen supreme
Zeus's girl, well, sea-foam girl, you got the tricks, please
break my heart and make me cry, not,
Beauty, my eyes out

Quick come on, since you once sometime
when? heard me call, me down here,
you up there answered and left old Zeus's
place in a hurry

in that boat that you drive reining those
fine fast birds, their wings whirring, you led them o-
ver the wide world from exo- through ion-
o- strato- to here

Those birds got you here, then you, Aphrodite,
whose smile just smiles through those lips and those eyes,
you asked again then what hurt me to call
you there again here

and what did I want most you do in my
madness "Which girl should I trick aphrodi-
siac love back to you," you asked, "that cheater,
ah, Sappho, her name?

Now she might flee you, soon she will pray on your name;
she flings back your gifts now, wait, she will take you
in love; she loves you not now, she will love you tomorrow
though will what she will"

Make it quick now, again, I really suffer,
Aphrodite, care fills me, fulfill my de-
sires, I (those things I want I really need) can't
do it without you

Like *Phainetai Moi*
from Sappho

Looks like Mr. Big Stuff, that one,
that guy with your eyes in his eyes
who hears in his ear your sweet nothings and
accepts them as his

and you tickling with laughter which, cross my
heart, makes dub dub dub lub lub dub lub of it.
Just a peek at you, I ... Dumb breath is all that
comes out of my mouth;

Iiii don't know what to say and flying
fire is under my skin now
I don't know what my eyes are for I begin now to
beat inside my ears

now my sweat runs and runs cold I twitch now now
I jerk now green from my eyes is all over me
I am barely enough me now to live.

Looks like I ——

An Horatian Toast

Drink! O Romans! Beat with your feet,
now free, on our ground that is freed.

Feast! O Romans! Feast from the couches
fitted for feasts of the gods by Mars' priests.

It was a sin when the Queen prepared death
for Roman men to uncork our fine wines.

Pestilent puff-breasted Egypt-bred dregs
courted her, drank with her drunk on her luck. But

burnt ships mixed her madness with wa-
tered flight from Octavian's hawk.

He the hunter and she the hare, this rare demon-
stration, O Caesar you'll snare.

Yet, unfainting at Antony's sword,
not veiling her fleet in an embracing shore,

she milked the asps at her breasts, *Salut*-
ed her palace, gave orders to death.

No Liburnian escort for her
past Caesar triumphant in Rome. Drink!

There Once was a Man from Verona

Aurelius and Furius, good friends
You'd follow Catullus to earth's ends

Just go to that girl
Who thinks she's the world
With her three hundred men
Who service her send-
Ing their slop up her hole
Till she cracks off each pole

If she mentions my name
Say she is to blame
For the stunned rose that won't bloom again

Ranking Aemilius

from Catullus

Holy Gods, the whole of him stinks –
   the hole where food enters; the hole where it leaves – Aemilius
might swap them about. Yet the truth of the stench is
   it's sweeter below, for his seat has no teeth and the teeth
for his meat are each half a foot over a foot,
   carried upon grey inveterate pallets, no gums
holding fast. When he laughs, he flaps open, portraying
   a she-mule who puddles the dust of a summer gone sour.
He has his women and thinks he's quite comely,
   and he's never been given to tend to the back of a grinding-wheel's
drudge-ass. Don't we think, yes we do, that the woman
   who knows him dines on the refuse the hanging man leaves?

Brother

> *Multas per gentes ... frater*
> CATULLUS

Driven through people and people and places
   I am come to this terrible service   brother
so I might give you your last gift   the death gift
   might talk to your ashes   might listen in vain for their voice
Since your life took you from me   seized you
   unjust   brother   misery   took you from me
now   as we were taught by our parents   here
   I offer my last gift   a death gift
take it   wrapped only in brotherly tears
   and always   my brother   now I have found you   farewell

Missing Brother, Missing Son

When we'd agreed you were gone
We spoke your name loudly
And often
Shouted it out to anyone who had known you
Or met you

Lost in a crowd
We'd find reasons to spit it out
Into the eyes of just anyone

For Them and Their Son

Thirty years. He does not age.
They know his hair, his weight,
How he turned out just three days
Before he'd turn twenty.

They know his hair, his weight,
His gait – off his toes. But not
If he turned twenty
Once he'd mailed that postcard.

His gait – off his toes – but not
If he could no longer walk
Once he'd mailed that postcard;
Struck by a car or the idea to run

Away, he could no longer walk
With their memories for company. (He'd be
Struck by a car or the idea to run
Were he someone who is not my son.)

With their memories for company, he'd be
Trying for thirty years to return.
(Were he someone who is not my son,
I still could not decide.)

Trying for thirty years to return!
Just how he turned out
They still will not decide.
Thirty years and he does not age.

Sentence

She told me I'd said this
 Bru ha shu on
as my first sentence

In all of the time since she told me,
only just (slow as I am), has it come to me now,
that she probably then, and throughout those years,
they, had fed me the words

 His little shoe is on his piggies
 Our little boy blue is here at home
 One day the feet he wears will take him
 Wave, bye-bye Brucey, bye-bye shoe

When one day came, it took a year to know it
We were stymied each then in our going on any more,
and by and by slow, as if we'd read the story how,
we waived each our lives their living

Katastrophe

Here I have been out-Peneloping Penelope –
though not a husband, yet a brother,
and I've thirty-five years to her twenty,
no suitors, and about my life the loosed ends fray.
On the weekend, the last of us, me,
was reading in the sunshine from his schoolboy copy
as Odysseus makes himself known bit by bit.
From the right, not an eagle from Zeus,
but a lady-bug, traveling bug, far from her home,
rifles the pages ahead, flies from me, taking
the shape of the wind.
Penelope questions the stranger.
He is tricked into the tale of the bedpost.
She knows him. Hurrah.

And then grief (and I quote): Penelope speaks –
                              Think
what difficulty the gods gave: they denied us
life together in our prime and flowering years,
kept us from crossing into age together.

In his schoolboy pen he'd marked
(just the sixth mark in the book) these lines.
He'd bracketed the four together,
as well as the inside two (those twice).
I had to turn my face from Ithaka,
and marvel at this, a sign, the first
through all these years, that he'd know of our cowls of sorrow,
and knowing, would not have bid us wear them,
and so, he is dead, dead decades ago,
could not have let us suffer.

    Had the gods not been rinsed from our world long ago
    It might have been wayfinder Hermes in lady-bug sandals
    Marking that passage while feast turned to massacre under my eyes.
    But the boy marked the passage, and he is dead now I know:

Son of once-adamant mother, self-abjected father.
They never bewailed at his bier, nor I.

Or, you, O my brother, made hidden farewell
On the margins of our fortune. Content.
Your passage craftily marked, our lives clanging upon us.

All Gone

Jimmy was born to nod *yes* and shake *no*
Each of the children knew him a good friend
The boy, then the girl, taught him to nod-shake
For questions most often were puzzling and fierce

Their parents agreed "Our children are clever"
Though this trick was more witkin than wit
Still, the children grew clever in cleverer ways
While Jimmy stayed mute and unschooled

Jimmy, dear Jimmy, in Nitey Nite clothes still
Come out of the toy chest, Come nod-shake for me
    Brucie's gone missing
    And Daddy, I found him's, gone silly
    (He tried to breathe plastic and all his breath's gone)
    Mommy can walk and can talk, little more
But I can still nod-shake like when we first met

Jimmy, sweet Jimmy, you still, too, can nod-shake
I'll wash your sweet clothing, and you, if I may
    Now your left arm's just come off
    And your leg, as I hold you
    And the bears in the toy chest must miss you
    But I, Jimmy Jimmy, have no one to teach me
Or think that I'm clever, I'm less whole than you now

I'll put you back now with the bears in your dry clothes
I'm sorry I hurt you, I know you're not mad
For you knew my beginning and brother and father
And mother (I told her I saw you today) smiled (I think
She remembered) when I brought up the nod-shake

The air of today is a danger, I'm sorry
I'd thought we might dance by the light of the moon
Your lashes have not lost their beauty
I'm lost Jimmy, tell me, a nod or a shake
Tell me tell me now what I must do

Song Sung after a Dirge

Isn't it so, old man, isn't it so?
I think you do know, old man, you had to go.
    You knew if you stayed with us
    You couldn't but raise a fuss
        That I couldn't stand.

Yes it was sad, old man, yes I'm still sad.
Were I a balladeer, I'd sing you as mad
    Deprived of his sweet love's health
    He madly killed himself
        Yet we had a plan.

You wrapped round your head, old man, to keep out the air
And sealed up the running car, just as I feared
    And just as I hoped you would
    You did. You did it. Ah good.
        You stayed not your hand.

The Keys and My Mother

He cares, my father, for everything
and I am to care so, too.
I laugh at his caring
and I am a cause for his care.
I learn to care as he does
and I am a case under care.
Ending his cares, he left the hedges cut,
and the keys and my mother to me.

You May Have the Body

Even diminished, she knew when I said
he is dead that he'd done it. Me too.
I knew it would be in the car, yet
I thought it would be by the car, not that
bag over his head (to make sure he'd be dead)
that the coroner said was the sole cause of death.

The coroner knew why I, without knowledge,
reasoned the car be the cause, yet
my father contained CO_2, not CO.
The science was something like that when
I called to explain the death report was wrong.

He'd have thought it all through, except for me,
who'd given him the time, who knew where
and knew that he must, who sat with the bag-
headed body and held his rigor-strong arm.

The mood is gone.
                        I know still I hated
that bag and my mother, who lived on
with the illness that killed him. They told me
he went whole with his eyes to science, but
I've never bothered to get the receipt.

Familiar Rhymes

How naughty to run the car with a hose
      Returning the fumes
      To the man in the car
How lonely to sit in the fume-ridden car
    Alone on a Wednesday morning

How silly to end with your head in a bag
      A white plastic bag
      The end of your life
How awful to get the sack in the end
    All done on a Wednesday morning

How long can we waste our breaths in our griefs
      Pretending the world
      Has yet to know griefs
The car, hose, that Wednesday, the man in the bag
    Have outspent hours they're due of the morning

What You Did

For my father, ten and then twenty years after

Oh, they would have been proud of you,
had they seen this, your home and its yard.

So, you weren't the genius
you once seemed you might be,
and you were ever the odd man out,
no matter with whom, yet
what a life you made, in part made for me,
in our green yard and its home for us four.

Millenniums of wants laid wall-to-wall,
we had color and shade in the yard.
Attached was a one-car garage so secure
no harm could leave it and enter the house
or anyone racing through it to find you,
unless it was harm to make me stand then outside,
stupidly smashing windows,
as if the ancient miasma you'd summoned
were only mists of time to be dispersed,
and so, then, you, restored
by the yet still vital air of that day.

Us Out

    I've all but given up, you know.
    Shut it down
    all but completely.

I didn't shut the running motor.
It's not right that you weren't there.
I'm the girl and I'm the youngest.
Where were you to tear the bag
that really killed him, not the car?

    Shut my mouth
    and shut my wanting.
    Shut behind polite and *mustn't*.

I could have shut her off and didn't.
I kept her as a tended nightmare.
She kept coins because you had.
Someone paid-for wiped her off.

    Shut out love because I loved you.
    Shut off growth because …
    who knows?

He must have been something to win her then,
when she was a glorious girl, and he
wasn't yet our sad raging father.
Where were you when I lost his body
to science or garbage? I don't know where it went.

    Where were –
    when you shut the door –
    you when you shut us out?

The family of Karp ran a school for itself
What are all those fish that lie gasping on the strand?
                                                W B Yeats

People won't like if you look at them bold
People won't like you if you don't do as you're told
People not us may do as they may
but one slip from you, daughter, will end in dismay
I'll curb you, I'll niggle, I'll make you feel small
though you're graceful and gentle, with the best brains of all
You have a sweet look to you
                        I'll make you think you should hide
for I know that women are too filled with pride
and they pluck and they shave and they cancel their smells
Don't make a good living, know nothing too well
(I once too had young vigor
but now see the world bigger)
Don't threaten, don't show off, don't do as you do
They'll hate you for Marcia, they'll hate you for Jew
Disappear if you're able, if you're not, you should be
I got lost in my growing – don't be happier than me
    You should suffer
                You should squirm
    You should try less hard to learn
Look at me
           I must teach how you'll feel when despised
We are nothing, not this family, you must see through their eyes

The House in Repair

You trained me well. When I first moved back,
I still felt like a guest in your house.
I hired the man you'd hired,
and he kept up the lawn much as he'd kept it for you.
He cut those last-chance hedges twice a summer.
Slowly, I change things.

I painted the house first in pinks
and now in a spectrum of orange and brown,
with the roof the same.
A banker who'd cared that you died
told me the roof was a worry to you,
but I took my time and am glad.
With the old bricking in front, the whole
set into the green that she'd planted around us,
it's warm and itself and now mine, your house.

I chose beautiful paper for the walls, which was hung
only half-right. I had to buy a new dryer, and did.
My first repair was just after the day,
to the last-hope glass I'd smashed with a rock,
not knowing you put on a bag once the hedges were done.

I'm a PhD now and the work is so sparse
that I cut the lawn and try to, the hedges,
now over my head and my reach.
Ever since the dryer sparked out in a flood,
I've hung the washing across the basement.
The new sump pump pumps hard,
and the window it drains through
is patched with some tiling
I can almost place from before.

Something happened during the painting.
The windows now mustn't be opened;
the old casement cranks barely work anymore.
It's not what you would have fussed over –
not paint on the to-and-fro arms or too thick at the edges –
but as if once I'd got it burnished,
the house, as I'd done years ago to my peril,
in its passing to me, shuddered,
so to hold in all of the air that sang once out from you.

Now I Lay Me

Over
      and over and over
Baby comes to take on the ogre.

She tries the mountain that she dreamt
when on rubber sheets she slept.
Baby in her big girl bed
held the dream as if it said,
not fear of something being there,
but fear of no one ever near,
   feared Baby.

Though not yet knowing life got lived,
it was as if she'd dreamt a gift
   of future must.
Poor BaBaby, could she know
how a thing not yet would go?

It stayed as truth, that dreamt-of climb,
and then she learnt that life was time,
and tried to think she was not meant
to be, nor was, an isolate.

Ogre, ogre, life's near over.

ABOUT THE AUTHOR

Author Photo by Peppa

Marcia Karp has published poems and translations in journals and anthologies in England and America, including *The Times Literary Supplement; Harvard Review; The Guardian; Partisan Review; The Word Exchange: Anglo-Saxon Poems in Translation* (Norton); and *Joining Music with Reason: 34 Poets, British and American, Oxford 2004-2009* (Waywiser). She taught literary and editorial matters at Boston University after earning graduate degrees there.

www.ingramcontent.com/pod-product-compliance
Lightning Source LLC
Chambersburg PA
CBHW031121080526
44587CB00011B/1063